STANDARD

PROGRAM BOOK

compiled by

Pat Fittro

Cincinnati, Ohio

Standard Publishing, Cincinnati, Ohio
A division of Standex International Corporation
© 2000 Standard Publishing

ISBN 0-7847-1176-3

Contents

Easy

A Welcome
Iris Gray Dowling

We're so glad you stopped by
    today—
  It's no accident you know;
We have wonderful news for you,
  God still loves you wherever
      you go.

Special Day
Cora M. Owen

This is a very special day,
And all of us are glad to say,
    Happy Easter!

Like He Said
Mary Ann Green

Jesus rose from the dead
Exactly like He said.

He Lives
Dolores Steger

He lives! He's taken sin away!
He's risen! Joy! It's Easter Day!

Tree
Mary Ann Green

He died upon a cruel tree
To bring salvation rich and free.

Easter Comes
Dolores Steger

Easter comes just once a year,
But the risen Christ is always
  here.

God's Love
Iris Gray Dowling

God gave His Son to us,
  Because of His great love;
He knew He'd die on the cross,
  That's why He came from above.

It's Time
Dolores Steger

It's time to praise;
  It's time to sing;
Oh, joy, He lives,
  The risen King.

God's Own Son
Mary Ann Green

The earth trembled and only
    darkness
  Came from the sun.
Indeed the One hanging on the
    tree
  Was God's own Son.

Easter's Here
Margaret Primrose

Easter's here
  So I came to say,
I hope you will have
  A lovely day.

Let's Celebrate
Margaret Primrose

Let church bells ring;
  Let children sing;
Let everyone bring
  Praises to our King.
    It's Easter!

Dark Clouds, Bright Sun
Dolores Steger

See the dark clouds as they cover
    the sky,
Knowing, today, that our Savior
    must die;
See the bright sun and the
    warmth that it gives,
Knowing, today, that the Lord
    ever lives.

Love
Mary Ann Green

When upon that rugged tree
My Savior died for you and me.
He brought salvation rich and
    free
God's great love has redeemed
    me.

Calvary's Love
Iris Gray Dowling

So much love was shown to me,
  As Jesus died on the tree;
He took my sins on Himself,
  As He suffered on Calvary.

Why?
Iris Gray Dowling

Why did Jesus love me so?
That's the answer I don't know;
He was the only perfect one,
That's why God gave His only
    Son.

This Is the Day
Dolores Steger

In gentle breeze the lilies sway,
  Somehow they know this is the
    day
To praise, rejoice, and so they
    wave,
  For Christ has risen from the
    grave.

The Thorn of Sin
Dolores Steger

The Lord has risen from His tomb,
  Hosannah! Praises sing;
In His shed blood, the thorn of
    sin
  Has lost its evil sting.

Thank Him
Margaret Primrose

Songs of praise to the living Lord
  And a story that is ever new
Remind us that once again it is
    time
  To thank Him that the story is
    true.
              Christ is risen!

I Know
Carolyn R. Scheidies

*(Hold up picture of a heart with a
cross in the center.)*

I know Jesus loves me,
  And this is how I know.
Jesus died and rose again,
  Because He loves me so.

It's a Happy Day
Cora M. Owen

Jesus lives,
Life He gives,
What a happy day!
He arose,
Gladness shows,
It's a happy day!

Three Crosses
Dolores Steger

On Golgotha's hill I see
  Crosses there, they number
    three;
Just one stands for victory
  The one where Jesus died for
    me.

The Cave
Dolores Steger

The cave is dark and empty now,
  Within it's always night;
But from it rose on Easter morn,
  The Lord, the Prince of Light.

Our King
Mary Ann Green

God sent His Son
The only one
Who could die on a tree
To forgive you and me.
Jesus is our king
Our salvation to bring.

7

Medium

He Now Lives
Cora M. Owen

He was once dead, but now He
   lives,
   Alive forevermore!
Death cannot claim my Lord again.
   Of that I'm very sure.

Because He lives, I too can live.
   This truly, I believe.
And I'm alive forevermore.
   His life I now receive.

I Love Jesus
Cora M. Owen

I love Jesus
Because He gives to me,
Life for eternity.
He lives forevermore!

I love Jesus,
And gladly I will sing,
Because He is my king,
Who lives eternally.

I love Jesus,
Because He lives today,
And He will live always,
Alive forevermore!

Placed
Dolores Steger

He's placed on a cross,
Then He's placed in a tomb,
Where He patiently waits there
   alone
For that morning to come
When He rises to be
Placed, by God, on His heavenly
   throne.

Why Jesus Died
Margaret Primrose

Jesus' cross was not made of gold.
I think it was rough and knotted
   and old.
There He hung and was left to die,
But He willingly suffered so that
   you and I
Can know Him as Savior and
   know Him as Friend
And share real joy that will never
   end.

I Believe
Margaret Primrose

I've never walked where Jesus
   walked
   Nor traveled to distant lands.
I've never seen His empty tomb
   Nor felt His nail-scarred hands.

Yet I believe He bled and died,
   Then rose again from the dead.
And I believe He'll come again,
   For that is what He said.

I'll Wear a Smile
Margaret Primrose

I don't like bows and ruffles;
  I never dress in lace.
What I really want you to see
  Is a smile I wear on my face.

For this is the day we remember
  The day that Jesus arose,
And a smile is much more
    important
  Than new or costly clothes.
      Happy Easter!

New Life in Christ
Iris Gray Dowling

When Jesus died on the cross
  I know it was for me.
On the third day He arose,
  The light my blinded eyes could
    see.

Now I say with many more—
  "I know my Savior lives."
What a change in me He made—
  New life He freely gives!

The Choice
Dolores Steger

Fluffy duck or soft, stuffed chick,
Let me see; which shall I pick
As my favorite Easter toy?
Which shall give me comfort, joy?
Umm? The choice is not so hard;
I'll choose the Lamb, the Lamb of
  God.

Easter Joy and Peace
Cora M. Owen

There is a reason to have joy,
  A risen Savior reigns,
And He's alive forevermore,
  In Heaven's great domain.

There is a reason to have peace,
  The risen Savior gave,
He meant it for His loved and
    own,
  When He rose from the grave.

God's Son
Iris Gray Dowling

At the cross of Calvary,
  Where they crucified God's Son;
Many knelt and cried nearby,
  'Til they heard Him say, "It's
    done!"

Not knowing all He meant—
  That salvation from sin was
    won;
Their saddened hearts were
    cheered,
  When alive they saw God's Holy
    One.

Why Did He Come?
Iris Gray Dowling

The babe of Bethlehem
  Was born so He could die;
He lived and taught the crowds
  But people asked the reason
    why.

To the cross and the grave He
    went
  So salvation's gift could be free.
Now the choice is mine to make
  His arms are open to me.

Come and See
Cora M. Owen

"Come and see," the angel said,
"Christ is risen from the dead,"
"He is not here, for He arose."
Now that news you must disclose.

"Go and tell," that He's alive,
"Go and tell," His life will thrive,
"Go and tell, He is not here."
Now there is no need to fear.

Power and Life
Cora M. Owen

God showed all His power when
  He raised Christ from the grave,
Life itself came forth again
  With wondrous pow'r to save.

Life could not stay in the tomb,
  Could not be buried long,
In the darkness, in the gloom
  For He is light and song.

Such Gladness
Cora M. Owen

Angels were glad,
  Disciples too,
When Jesus rose
  For me, for you.

Women rejoiced,
  I am glad too,
For Jesus lives
  For me, for you.

He Gave
Mary Ann Green

Jesus came to earth
Through a humble birth.
It was through great love
He came from above.
He grew straight and tall
Taught rabbis and all.
He willingly gave
His life on a tree
That we could be free
Through all eternity.

Footprints
Dolores Steger

Footprints lead from Galilee
  Up to Golgotha's hill,
Then rest within a darkened
    tomb,
  Sealed tight; they stay there till
Emerging, they continue on
  To vividly display
Salvation's path to Heaven's
    realm,
  The Truth, the Life, the Way.

Easter Celebration
Wanda E. Brunstetter

Easter baskets filled with treats,
Smiling children, the morning
   greets.
Heavenly Son-shine from up
   above,
Glistening on each one with love.
Though eggs and treats are lots of
   fun,
We celebrate Easter because of
   God's Son!

Easter Is a Promise
Dolores Steger

Chicks and eggs and bunnies,
  At Eastertime you see;
The baskets filled with goodies
  Are pretty as can be.

But Easter is a promise,
  In knowing Jesus, He
Died for our salvation
  And rose to set us free.

Time to Praise Jesus
Margaret Primrose

Easter bunnies, Easter hats—
Easter this and Easter that.
These are not what the day is
   about;
They're not the reason to stand
   and shout.
Christ is risen, and it's time to
   sing
Our highest praises to the risen
   King.

A Reason to Shout
Margaret Primrose

Easter lilies in gowns of white
  Are standing straight and tall;
They make me want to do the
  same
  Although I may be small.

So I won't slump and wear a
   frown,
  Nor forget what this day is
   about,
But I will smile as I look at you,
  And I may even shout—Happy
   Easter! *(May cup hands around
   mouth.)*

Surprise
Dolores Steger

In winter, flowers hide in the
   ground,
Until the spring when they
   abound.
And on the land, before my eyes,
They wave in gentle winds;
   surprise!

In darkness, He hid in a tomb;
On Easter morn, He left the gloom
Of cavern dark, and did arise,
God's promise to fulfill; surprise!

Difficult

Follow the Shepherd
Tobi Anne Tate

As sheep we have all gone astray,
  Unwilling at times to be led;
Praise God, there is hope for today,
  If we follow the Shepherd instead.
Separation from God cannot be,
  So Christ willingly died for us all;
He victoriously rose from the dead,
  To redeem us from the curse of
    the law. *(Galatians 3:13)*
When you feel as if you've lost
    your way,
  Or you question where you have
    been led;
If darkness has become your day,
  Call out to the Shepherd instead.
    (Jeremiah 33:3)
Like a lost sheep returned to the
    flock,
  We are welcomed with love pure
    as gold;
The Good Shepherd is our solid
    rock,
  And we are as sheep in His fold.
In our prayers, we ask for His
    counsel,
  And wisdom when we don't
    understand;
The Lord favors the people of His
    pasture,
  And blesses the sheep of His
    hand. *(Psalm 95:7)*

What Will Easter Morning Bring?
Dolores Steger

Gentle breezes,
Birds that sing?
What will Easter morning bring?

Cloudless skies,
The flowers of spring?
What will Easter morning bring?

Bunnies, chicks,
And egg-hunting?
What will Easter morning bring?

Choir music,
Church bells ring?
What will Easter morning bring?

What will Easter morning bring?
It will bring the Savior, King.

Why I Like Easter
Margaret Primrose

I like Easter dresses,
  Hats and new white shoes.
I like hunting eggs
  And singing in long full pews.

But the very best thing about
    Easter
  Isn't candy or pretty clothes;
It isn't just the things
  That others may suppose.

It's thanking Jesus for the love
  That led Him to choose the cross
And thanking God that He arose
  When it seemed that all was loss.

Miracles of Love

Iris Gray Dowling

The sinless, perfect Son of God
  Came down from Heav'n to die
A shameful death on Cavalry's
    cross,
  While friends and loved ones
    wondered why.

There were miracles to come—
  When soldiers sealed the tomb—
In three short days they saw
    God's power—
  He conquered death's dark
    gloom.

I'll tell you of another miracle—
  Yes, God has changed my sinful
    heart—
Transforming me to show His
    love
  And work so others find a start.

He Is Risen

Iris Gray Dowling

Devoted men took Jesus down
  From the cross to the cold, dark
    tomb;
Sadness filled those friendly
    hearts,
  Even the sky had an eery gloom.

Sunday morning was different,
    though—
  The tomb was filled with angel's
    light;
The stone had been rolled away,
  Yet no one passed the guards
    that night.

There was a joy that none could
    express,
  When the angel said, "He is not
    dead!
He is not here; He's risen!
  Don't you remember what He
    said?"

Jesus

Dolores Steger

The cross is set
  Upon the hill
The crowd is there
  To see the kill
Of Jesus.

They shout aloud;
  They laugh; they jeer;
With scorn they cry
  As He draws near.
It's Jesus.

To cross He's bound;
  They watch Him die,
As darkened clouds
  Invade the sky
O'er Jesus.

Perhaps one day
  They will conceive
His death means life
  If they believe
In Jesus.

The Lord, Our Lord
Dolores Steger

The Lord, our Lord, is coming
    now,
So wave palms high and lowly
    bow,
And as He passes, praises sing,
Hosannah, it's the King, the King.

No royal robes upon Him rest,
He wears no gold or jeweled
    crown,
He rides on donkey meek and
    mild,
Hosannah! He's arrived in town.

He's come to die for all our sins
And then to rise so we may live
With Him in an eternal peace;
Hosannah! Praises to Him give.

A Wonderful Story
Margaret Primrose

Three crosses on a lonely hillside
    Spread their news of a dreadful
      day
While the innocent Man in the
    middle
    Hung there with little to say.

But three little words He said
    Are as important as they can be,
For His prayer was, "Father, for-
    give them,"
    And was meant for you and me.

What a wonderful story it is
    For Jesus arose from the grave,
And I'm glad for the love He
    offers
    As well as His power to save.

The Cross and the Cave
Dolores Steger

The cross on which they crucified
The Lord, the cross on which He
    died,
Is empty now, there to remain
A symbol of His suffering, pain.

The cave in which His body lay
Until that third momentous day
Is empty now, a sign that He
Lives; He lives eternally.

The cross is empty, as the cave;
They represent the life He gave
And then regained, to set us free
And be with us eternally.

Take His Hand
Dolores Steger

Take my hand and come with me
To a hill, to Calvary,
A crucifixion there to see,
A King about to die.

Take my hand and come my way
To a cave where once He lay,
Until the wondrous Easter day,
He rose toward sunlit sky.

Take His hand and follow when
He claims you, His child, and
    then,
Just take His hand; rejoice again,
Our Savior reigns on high.

No End

Dolores Steger

A crown of thorns they place on
  Him,
  To wooden cross He's nailed;
With insults and with ridicule,
  His being is assailed.

They watch Him suffer endlessly,
  With mocking shouts and cries,
They taunt Him, call Him
  criminal,
  Three hours till He dies.

And with His blood upon their
  hands,
  They fail to comprehend,
His death brings life forevermore,
  In Him there is no end.

Symbols

Dolores Steger

Chickens and bunnies and bright
  eggs may suit
You as the symbols of Easter:
  they're cute.
So are the ducks and the baskets
  piled high
With treats overflowing and
  tempting the eye,
But they're only with us a
  moment or two;
We need some symbols that last
  ages through,
So, I say the cross and the crown
  are the best;
They'll surely endure and outlast
  all the rest.

Imagining

Margaret Primrose

When Jesus rose from the dead,
  Did the birds wake up and sing?
Did even the breeze in the meadow
  Join in praise to the living King?

Did the clouds all disappear
  As the sun climbed out of its bed,
And the music of the rippling
  brook
  Praise God that He rose from the
  dead?

I know it's easy to imagine
  A lot that may not be true,
But I'm glad for a living Savior,
  And I think that you are too.
    Happy Easter!

Resurrection Time

Cora M. Owen

Spring is resurrection time,
  When all things are as new,
Trees and blossoms come alive
  They make a pleasant view.

Birds all build their nests again,
  As they break into song,
Nature has been fast asleep,
  All through the winter long.

As the flowers come to life,
  And grass begins to grow,
It is resurrection time,
  And Jesus lives, we know.

Getting Ready For Easter
Margaret Primrose

I can get ready for Easter
  Without any fancy new clothes,
And I'm trying to do a little
  With birdseed and a garden
     hose.

I can feed my feathered friends
  To help them sing for us all.
I can also water the flowers
  To keep them standing tall.

But far far more important,
  I can stop to bow my head
While I talk to the wonderful
     Savior
  Who died but rose from the
     dead.

(Prays) Thank You, Lord, for Your
     world
  And the welcome signs of spring
That make us think of Your
     goodness
  And encourage us to sing.

But they are only reminders
  Of Your great and marvelous
     love.
We thank You most for the Savior
  Who lives in Heaven above.

God Had a Plan
Margaret Primrose

How does a tiny seed
  Spring from its garden bed?
Who tells a tight little bud
  To open and show its head?

When the birds are flying north,
  How do they know where to go?
Who keeps the sun in its place
  And helps it melt the snow?

I believe I know the answer—
  God planned that all this should
     be
Just as He planned that Jesus
  Would die for you and me.

And if God can guide a robin
  To the tree where it hatched in a
     nest,
If He can water a daisy,
  Then clothe it in its best,

If He can make the sun rise
  And keep it in the sky,
Then I can come to Jesus
  And be sure that He is nigh.

Yes, I can know for certain
  That the Easter story is true,
And that Jesus is now in Heaven
  Preparing it for me and you.

Remember the Cross
Cora M. Owen

Remember the cross that stood on
  a hill,
  A curse, a blot, what a shame!
Remember its shadow against the
  sky,
  At Calvary when darkness came.

Remember the Christ who died
    on that cross,
  And sin for all sinners became;
Remember the blood that ran
    from His side,
  A flow for all people to claim.

Remember His hands they nailed
    to the cross,
  Forever to bear all the scars.
Remember His brow when
    crowned with the thorns,
  His face with its pain and its
    mars.

Remember He finished His work
    that day,
  Fulfilled all God's perfect plan.
Remember how lovingly, freely
    He gave,
  Providing redemption for man.

Eternity
Dolores Steger

He's working His miracles there
    on the road,
  Though certainly most do not
    see,
As they wave their palms while
    He draws near,
  The Savior that He'll come to be.

He's working His miracles there
    on the cross,
  Though very few can realize,
As they laugh and cheer while He
    submits,
  A King such as He never dies.

He's working His miracles there
    in the tomb,
  Some mourners attending the
    grave,
Sadly unknowing He'll rise again,
  The Lord who man from sin will
    save.

He's working His miracles on
    earth today
  He's risen to show everyone
He's Lord and Savior, King of all
    kings,
  He's the gift from the Father, the
    Son.

Easter Morn
Lillian Robbins

When the sun comes up on Easter
morn,
  I think of a day long ago.
The friends of Jesus had watched
  Him die.
  They surely had loved Him so.

They had talked with Him so
  many times
  And walked the roads by His
  side.
Now they could only reverently
  bow
  As the women sorrowfully cried.

Never was one as great as He.
  His life brought joy to man.
The words of truth He spoke each
  day
  Revealed to all God's plan.

Enemies of Jesus put Him to
  death;
  They thought their scheme had
  won.
They just didn't fully understand
  at all,
  The power through Christ,
    God's Son.

Death for Jesus was a moment of
  time
  From creation to His ultimate
  reign
In Heaven by God on His
  personal throne
  Where nothing is ever the same.

As the earthquake shook, graves
  opened that day;
  The viewers had a different feel.
At last the doubtful at the foot of
  the cross
  Could know that Jesus was real.

The women had known when the
  Sabbath came
  God's law they must obey.
They would wait to bring their
  herbs and spice
  At the dawn on the following
  day.

Sadly they went as they walked
  the path,
  To Arimathaea and Joseph's land
To reach the grave where Jesus
  was laid.
  Provided by this caring man.

"How shall we move away that
  stone?"
  The women did contemplate.
They knew their strength wasn't
  nearly enough
  To lift so heavy a weight.

They need not worry their minds
  at all;
  God's plan would be complete.
Amazed they were, and much
  afraid;
  With the angel of God did meet.

"Don't be afraid," the angel said,
  Assurance to them he gave.
"Why seek the living among the
  dead?
  Jesus arose from this grave.

"Just look here in this new hewn
    tomb;
  See proof He's no longer dead.
Remember how He spoke the
    words in life.
  He arose as He had said.

"Go to His disciples and speak
    the truth,
  He travels to Galilee.
There they will be so happily
    blessed
  When His face they are able to
    see."

With exuberant joy the women
    went,
  The resurrection to proclaim.
Jesus was alive forevermore;
  Conquered death and sin and
    shame.

For people throughout all the
    years,
  The reality is still quite true.
Jesus died and arose again the
    third day,
  Paid the price for me and you.

On the cross where He bled, suf-
    fered and died,
  The darkest day that ever has
    been
Became the blessing for all
    mankind;
  The Lord Jesus defeated all sin.

Today we thank Him and honor
    His name.
  Praise God for His marvelous
    grace.

We'll prepare ourselves for that
    final day
  To see Him face to face.

To each of you who have come to
    share,
  We have this message to say,
Be thankful to God and honor His
    Son
  On this joyful Resurrection Day.

I Can Talk to Jesus
Margaret Primrose

Whether I'm happy or feel all
    alone,
I can't talk to Jesus on a cellular
    phone.
I can't send Him e-mail nor even
    a card,
But talking to Jesus is not really
    hard.

I'm glad I can pray just
    anywhere—
In a car, in a plane or a rocking
    chair.
I can talk to Jesus, our wonderful
    King
About all that's important or
    some little thing.

So now that I have something
    special to say—*(Bows head.)*
Thank You, Jesus, for this Easter
    Day.
Thanks that for us You suffered
    and bled,
And thanks to God, You rose
    from the dead.

They're Waving Palms

Dolores Steger

They're waving palms, but do
   they know
That to Golgotha's hill He'll go,
There to suffer, bound and tied,
On a cross, be crucified.

They're waving palms, and hear
   them say,
Hosannah without knowing they
Soon will see Him buried there
In a cave of dark despair.

They're waving palms; He enters
   town;
His life for them He will lay
   down;
They're waving palms; one day
   they'll see
He offers them eternity.

What I'd Like to Do

Margaret Primrose

I like to skip and hop and run;
I like to play in the morning sun.
It's fun to skate on thick smooth
   ice
And walking in the rain with a
   friend is nice.

But if I could choose what I'd like
   best,
It would be to stroll with a
   heavenly guest.
I'd like to sit at His nail-scarred
   feet.
Listening to His stories would be
   a treat.

So I thank the Lord for that first
   Easter Day
When He won the victory over
   death and decay.
Because of that both you and I
Can live forever with Him in the
   sky.

He Never Dies

Dolores Steger

Wave the palms, He's entering
Into town; it is the King.
Hallelu, hosanna sing;
Sad, so soon, He dies.

Mourn Him, on the cross He's
   nailed,
And with taunts and jeers He's
   hailed,
Mocked, His spirit is assailed;
Sad, you see, He dies.

Then, to surely seal His doom,
In a place that's dark with gloom,
He's placed in a cavern tomb;
Now they know He dies.

There, in solitude He lies
For three days, then breaks His
   ties;
It's God's promise that He rise,
And, no, never dies.

Exercises

E–A–S–T–E–R
Margaret Primrose

E is for everything Christ is—
　He's Savior, Guide and Friend.
He's Lord of all the big round
　world
And His love will never end.

A is for all, for all have sinned
　And need His pardoning grace,
But A is also for all it cost
　When He offered to die in our
　　place.

S is for the suffering that Jesus
　endured
　Though never once did He sin.
He gave himself to die for us
　In a battle He knew He would
　win.

T is for the tomb where Jesus was
　placed—
　Where His body was left to
　decay.
How tearful His mother and
　friends must have been
　As they watched, then turned
　away!

E is for eternal life,
　A gift that all may receive,
Though many who mourned the
　Savior's death
　Must have struggled hard to
　believe.

R is for the risen Lord
　And Resurrection Day.
How blessed are they who trust
　in Him
　And determine to obey!

*(May be spoken by six children, each
with a letter card.)*

Jesus Died for All
Margaret Primrose

First Child
Did Jesus have to die?
　Couldn't He have fled?
Were there no brave men to help
　Him
　In the multitudes He fed?

Second Child
Of course, He could have escaped,
　But He chose to die for man.
That means He thought of us all
　And had a perfect plan.

First Child
Do you mean He died for the
　soldiers
　Who nailed His hands and feet?
Did He even die for Judas,
　Whose kiss was full of deceit?

Second Child
Yes, Jesus died for us all—
　No matter what we have done.
We only have to confess
　And make Him Number One.

Heaven's Bells

Iris Gray Dowling

(An exercise for five children. Each holds an object or picture to illustrate the lines.)

Child 1: When Jesus came to earth,
The shepherds heard the angels sing.
(Show object to illustrate the manger scene.)

Child 2: At His death on Calvary's cross
Some tears were shed for this sad thing.
(Hold up a symbol of the cross.)

Child 3: But on His resurrection day
The angels had good news to bring;
(Show picture of angel at tomb.)

Child 4: "He is not here; He's risen as He said."
With joy His friends then tried to sing.
(Show picture of the open, empty tomb.)

Child 5: No one on earth heard Heaven's bells,
But I believe they had to ring.
(Hold a bell; ring it after the word "ring.")

Family Tree

Carolyn R. Scheidies

(Each person/group holds an appropriate card.)

1: C is for Christ crucified on the cross at Calvary.
2: R is for Remission of sins—the reason Jesus came for you and me.
3: O is for Outside the city, where they nailed Him to the tree.
4: S is for His Sacrifice as He gave His life to set us free.
5: S is for Jesus *(Pause.)* Son of God, who came as our Savior, you see,
1 & 2: To add us to His family tree,
3 & 4: And live with Him . . .
5: Eternally.
All: "For ye are all the children of God by faith in Christ Jesus"
(Galatians 3:26).

Song: "Jesus Loves Me" *(all three verses)*

Truth Revealed

Carolyn R. Scheidies

Group 1: First and second graders
Group 2: Third and fourth graders
Group 3: Fifth and sixth graders
(Optional: six individuals/groups of any age)

Scriptures are from the *New International Version* of the Bible.

All: "Christ Arose!" *(Group 3—verse 1, Groups 1 and 2—verse 2, All— verse 3.)*

Group 1 *(Carrying crosses.):*

First Graders:	Easter's about a Savior
	Whose love took Him to a cross.
	A Savior who gave His life,
	To offer forgiveness to the lost.
Second Graders:	So at this Easter season,
	Let the truth be revealed,
	For it's about a sacrificial death,
	And a tomb tightly sealed.

Verse: "For the Son of Man came to seek and to save what was lost" (Luke 19:10).

Song: "Just As I Am" *(verse 1)*

Group 2:

Third Graders:	Jesus left a throne, *(Manger picture.)*
	To be born in an animal stall,
	And lived a life of caring,
	Reaching out to one and all.
Fourth Graders:	He did not stop the people *(Christ on cross.)*
	Who crucified Him on the tree.
	For He knew His voluntary death
	Would set His people free.

Verse: "For God so loved the world that he gave his one and only Son, that whoever believes in him shall not perish but have eternal life. For God did not send his Son into the world to condemn the world, but to save the world through him. Whoever believes in him is not condemned, but whoever does not believe stands condemned already because he has not believed in the name of God's one and only Son" (John 3:16-18).

Song: "Tell Me the Story of Jesus" *(Verses 1 and 3)*

Group 3:

Fifth Graders:	Easter morning He broke the bonds *(Picture of open grave.)* Of death and hell and sin. Now Jesus offers abundant life To all who ask Him in.
Sixth Graders:	So let us bow this very day, *(Kneel.)* And give our hearts to He Who gave His life that we might know Forgiveness, hope and peace.

Verse: "I have come that they may have life, and have it to the full" (John 10:10).

Song: "My Hope Is in the Lord" *(Parts, all verses)*

All: "Christ the Lord Is Risen Today" *(Group 1—Verse 1, Groups 1 and 2—verse 2, Groups 1, 2 & 3—Verse 3, All groups and audience—verse 4. Have everyone stand for this song.)*

He Is Living!

Mary Rose Pearson

Our play is an imaginary story, but it is based on true events that we can read in the Bible. We begin in the home of Claudius, a Roman soldier living in Jerusalem in the days of Christ.

Characters:
Priscilla, a Roman woman
Tabitha, her young daughter
Claudius, Priscilla's husband and a Roman soldier
Marcus, a Roman soldier
Three Jewish women
Angel

Costumes: For the women and girls—Bible-time robes; for the soldiers— tight knee pants, short skirts over the pants, short-sleeved tops and helmets, all a gray color resembling metal; for the angel—a white robe

Setting: In a church sanctuary, place the home on the speaker's platform and the tomb in the choir loft or inside the baptistry with a curtain in front of it.

Scenes I and III: Inside the home of Claudius in Jerusalem, includes three simple chairs.

Scene II: Outside Jesus' tomb.

Scene I

Inside the home of Claudius. Priscilla and Tabitha enter and are seated.

Tabitha: Mother, this has been such a scary day! I hope Father comes home soon.

Priscilla: And so do I, Tabitha. I have been very frightened. I wonder what will happen next. *(She pauses.)* Listen! I hear footsteps. Maybe it's your father now. *(Claudius enters.)* Oh, it is you, Claudius. We're glad you're home.

Tabitha *(running to her father and hugging him)*: Oh, Father, it's been an awful day!

Claudius: I know. I have never known a day like it. *(They are seated.)*

Priscilla: Quickly! Tell us what is going on.

Claudius: The events of this day would be enough to vex the stoutest soldier. I wish I had never been on duty.

Priscilla: We heard loud noises in the night after you left. It sounded like crowds of people yelling.

Claudius: Yes, there was a huge mob. We soldiers could barely control them. The Jews here in Jerusalem had captured a fellow—Jesus by name. They put Him on trial, right then, in the night.

Tabitha: Jesus? Why, I know Him, Father. One day, when I was playing with my Jewish friends, Jesus passed by. They said He is called the Master, and He does many miracles.

Claudius (*scoffing*): Miracles? I doubt that.

Tabitha: They said He made a blind man see.

Claudius: It must have been a trick. I don't believe in miracles.

Tabitha: We ran to see Jesus, Father. Some men pushed us away and said not to bother the Master; but Jesus said, "Let the little children come to me."

Priscilla: That was very kind.

Tabitha: He had the kindest face I ever saw! I know He loves children. Why did the Jews want to capture Him?

Claudius: I don't know. Some cried one thing, and some another. They did agree He said He was the King of the Jews.

Priscilla: And they tried Him just for that? Surely they let Him go, didn't they?

Claudius: Oh, no! They cried for Barabbas, the robber, to be released, and for Jesus to be crucified.

Priscilla: What did Jesus say?

Claudius: That is the strange part. He did not say a word.

Tabitha: What did they do to Jesus, Father?

Claudius: Awful things. They scourged Him with a leather whip on His bare back until it was bloody. They put a purple robe on Him and made fun of Him. They put a crown of thorns on His head, spit in His face, and slapped Him.

Priscilla: Did you do any of those things, Claudius?

Claudius: Yes, at first; but Jesus never fought back or said a word. I couldn't go on. I never saw such a man!

Tabitha (*anxiously*): Did they let Him go then, Father?

Claudius: No. They led Him out of the city to Mount Calvary and nailed Him to a cross. He was crucified.

Tabitha (*appalled*): Crucified? Jesus crucified? Oh, Father!

Claudius: I wonder who He really was. He was so brave; and He prayed—yes, He prayed for us, who crucified Him.

Tabitha: That sounds just like what Jesus would do.

Claudius: Such strange things happened! It became dark as night for three hours, right in the middle of the day.

Tabitha (*shivering*): Ooh! It was dark here, too. And then there was an earthquake. I thought it was the end of the world. I was so scared!

Claudius: You're not the only one! Pilate told us soldiers to break the legs of the men on the three crosses. But when I came to Jesus, He was already dead.

Tabitha (*mournfully*): Oh, it is so sad! Jesus is dead.

Claudius: When I saw He was dead, I thrust a spear into His side; and blood and water came out. Who could this Jesus have been?

Tabitha: My friends told me He is the Son of God.

Claudius: Hmmm. Some of our soldiers said that too. (*He stands up.*) Well, I will eat some food and rest a little. Then I must stand guard at the tomb of Jesus. Pilate's orders.

Priscilla: Stand guard at the tomb? Why?

Claudius: The Jews think someone may steal Jesus' body. It seems Jesus said He would rise again if He was killed.

Tabitha (*gleefully*): Oh, maybe He will come ALIVE again!

Claudius: What foolishness! That could never happen. Still, I wish I had no part in this. But I am a Roman soldier. I will do my duty. (*The three leave.*)

Scene II

Outside the tomb. The curtain opens. The lights are dim. The angel is crouched down out of sight. Claudius and Marcus stand near the tomb.

Claudius (*stretching and yawning*): It's been a long night, Marcus! I'm glad it's nearly morning.

Marcus: This is the third day since Jesus was buried. I think Pilate and the Jews worried needlessly, Claudius. No one has come near this place.

(The angel rises up suddenly and a bright light shines on him.)

Claudius (*very alarmed*): Marcus—L-L-LOOK! Wh—who is THAT?

(Both men fall down. The lights darken and the angel crouches down again. Pause. The men get up and run out. Pause. The lights gradually brighten as the three women enter and go toward the tomb.)

Woman: Look, the stone is already rolled away! What can it mean?

(The angel appears and the bright light shines on him.)

Woman: Oh, look—LOOK! An ANGEL!
Other Women *(very frightened)*: Ohhh!
Angel: Don't be alarmed. You are looking for Jesus of Nazareth who was crucified. He has risen! He is not here.

(The women run offstage as the curtain is drawn.)

Scene III

Inside the home of Claudius. Claudius, Priscilla and Tabitha enter talking excitedly and are seated.

Priscilla: Tell us again, Claudius. You saw WHAT?
Claudius: Something strange—a ghost or an angel, maybe. Whatever it was, it was powerful. Why, Marcus and I fell down like dead men. When we came to our senses, the tomb of Jesus was empty—EMPTY, I say.
Priscilla: That's hard to believe.
Tabitha: I believe it. Jesus came alive, didn't He, Father?
Claudius: Well . . . don't breathe a word of this to anyone. The Jews paid Marcus and me a great sum of money to say Jesus' disciples came during the night and stole His body while we were asleep.
Tabitha: That's a lie, isn't it, Father?
Claudius: Yes. We never went to sleep. No matter what they make me say, they cannot change what I know. Nobody stole Jesus' body; but that tomb was empty, except for His clothes. These strange events trouble my mind greatly. Who could this Jesus be?
Tabitha: My friends said He is the Son of God.
Claudius: I can't understand it, but I believe it. Truly He is the Son of God. And He is not dead—HE IS LIVING!

(They leave.)

Optional ending: Read aloud Matthew 27:54. The soldiers at the cross of Jesus, after seeing the things that happened, did indeed say that Jesus was the Son of God.

Right On!
Dolores Steger

Characters and Costumes: Five youth, casually dressed

Time: The present, the day after Easter Sunday

Place: A living room or den

Set Requirements: Chairs for youth, other room furnishings (optional)

Music: Piano/organ/choir/tape

Youth sit chatting in chairs arranged center stage facing audience, as music "When Morning Gilds the Skies" plays. Youth 1 speaks when music stops.

Youth 1: So what did you guys do yesterday on Easter Sunday? Did you all have a good day?

Others: Wow! Yes! Super! Terrific!

Youth 1 *(to Youth 2)*: Tell us about it. What did you do that made the day so special?

Youth 2: I'd have to say it was going to the Easter egg hunt in the park. There must have been at least a hundred kids there. They divided us into groups by age and we had fifteen minutes to search for the eggs. They were plastic, of course, and they had little prizes inside. You know: candy, trinkets, pennies. After the hunt, they served refreshments and this crazy clown bunny entertained us. I was at the park most of the day.

Youth 3: Sounds neat!

Others: Really neat!

Youth 1 *(to Youth 3)*: What about your Easter? What did you do yesterday?

Youth 3: We spent the day at my Aunt Amy and Uncle Frank's house. All my cousins were there. Aunt Amy fixed a terrific meal for us: ham, potatoes, corn, beans, apple pie. I ate everything but the beans. The grown-ups did a lot of talking; but my cousins and I asked to be excused, and we played games on the computer, watched a couple of videos and managed to squeeze in a few games of tennis on the courts a block from Aunt Amy's house. My cousins are fun to be with. We had a great day.

Youth 4: I had a great day too.

Youth 1: What did you do?

Youth 4: We went to Fun World, that amusement place not far from town. The workers there were all dressed in Easter costumes: bunnies, chicks, eggs. The rides were out of this world. I went on every one of them. I got soaked on the waterwheel, but I won two prizes in an arcade game where I had to toss rings over the ears of rabbits.

Youth 5: What did you win?

Youth 4: A stuffed bear and a balloon that said, "Happy Easter."

Youth 5: You were lucky.

Youth 4: It took more skill than luck.

Others: Sure! Sure!

Youth 4: Anyway, I had a super Easter.

Youth 5: Me too, although it was very different from anything I'd ever done on Easter before.

Youth 2: How so?

Youth 5: Well, all the kids on my block got together in my backyard. We brought our Easter baskets with us and we made trades for the treats we wanted. I never saw so many chocolate bunnies and marshmallow chicks and jelly beans passing back and forth in my life. I cornered all the marshmallow chicks I could get.

Youth 3: What did you do with them?

Youth 5: Ate them. Ate them all. My stomach was upset last night but it was worth it, and I still have enough goodies left over to keep my stomach in orbit for weeks to come.

(Others laugh.)

Youth 4: It seems we all had a sensational Easter.

Youth 3: You bet! And I can't wait until it comes around again next year.

Youth 2: Wait a sec! Wait a sec! *(To Youth 1.)* You haven't told us what you did for Easter.

Others: Yeah! Yeah!

Youth 1: It was nothing at all like what you guys did.

Youth 2: No?

Youth 1: No. It was better. Much better.

Youth 3: So what was it?

Youth 4: Yeah. What did you do?

Youth 1: I had a perfect Easter day. I went to church.

Others: Church?

Youth 1: Yes. Church. We sang hymns praising God for the sacrifice of His Son so that we could be free from sin. We said prayers thanking

God for our Savior's resurrection which lets us know that we, too, can live eternally in Heaven with Him. The minister read from the Bible and told the story of Jesus' entry into Jerusalem, of His crucifixion, His burial and resurrection. Then he explained how important it is for us to know that Jesus' shed blood washed away our sins and that Jesus' resurrection gives us all the promise of eternal life.

Youth 2: That's heavy stuff.

Youth 1: Uh-huh.

Youth 2: Sounds a lot more important than going to an Easter egg hunt.

Youth 1: Uh-huh.

Youth 3: Or playing computer games or tennis.

Youth 1: Uh-huh.

Youth 4: Or winning prizes at Fun World.

Youth 1: Uh-huh.

Youth 5: Or stuffing your face with marshmallow chicks.

Youth 1: Absolutely.

Youth 2: It would seem the rest of us really dropped the ball. We missed out on the true meaning of Easter.

Youth 3: But we won't make that same mistake again, will we?

Youths 2, 4, 5: No! No!

Youth 3: Next year, we'll celebrate Easter as it should be celebrated. We'll go to church!

Others: Right on!

(Music of "When Morning Gilds the Skies" plays as participants take curtain call.)

Mother's Day

Welcome All Mothers
Iris Gray Dowling

Welcome all mothers and
    grandmothers, too,
So many people look up to you.
We've heard you sing and take
    time to pray,
As you went about God's work
    each day.

Her Stories
Cora M. Owen

My mother tells me stories
  The best I ever heard;
Because they are of Jesus
  And from God's holy Word.

Mother's Day
Dolores Steger

Mother's Day comes once a year,
  That's very plain to see,
But every day that passes, Mom,
  You mean much more to me.

My Mother Listens
Iris Gray Dowling

My mother is a special person,
  Who listens to me every day;
She also tries to understand—
  To her it is important what I say.

My Mother Helps
Iris Gray Dowling

My mother has a listening ear,
I know she's always near;
My mother's just the one I need,
Her words I really try to heed.

God Gave Us Mothers
Dolores Steger

God gave us mothers
  So there would be
A vision of His love
  For all to see.

Mothers Are Special
Dolores Steger

Mothers are special;
  They're gifts from above,
Reminding us all
  Of God's caring and love.

I Want to Please
Helen Kitchell Evans

Sure, my mother makes me
  Be good. Sure, I must mind.
But I want to please her
  Because she is so kind.

Oh, So True
Dolores Steger

God made mothers, it's oh, so
   true,
To be blessings for me and you.

A Little Card
Dolores Steger

Mom, I've made a little card
And, in it, I've tried really hard
To find the words so you may see
How very much you mean to me.

A Special Day
Helen Kitchell Evans

Spring slips in on gentle breezes
   (Slowly.)
  Bringing Mother's Day;
A time we each show extra love
   (Pause after each.)
  In some very special way.

Besides telling you my mother
  Really is a true winner
I've been saving from my
   allowance *(Pause.)*
  And I'm taking her out to
   dinner.

*(Underlined words need special
emphasis. This does not mean louder,
but pausing to give more expression
to these words.)*

Today's the Day
Cora M. Owen

Today's the day to celebrate,
  A day for a dear mother.
She's a very special one,
  Whose love is like no other.

Today's the day to let her know,
  How special she'll always be,
That love for her is very real,
  As you can plainly see.

Something About
A Mother
Cora M. Owen

There's something about a mother
Who loves the Word of God,
To Jesus she'll be so faithful
Her prayer life won't be flawed.

There's something about a mother,
Whose heart is full of love,
For she cares about her children
Like the Father up above.

Honor Mother
Cora M. Owen

Honor Mother every day,
  Special tribute to her pay.
As you're learning to obey
  Loving words, be sure to say.

Let your actions always be,
  What you'd like Mother to see,
Listen to her carefully,
  With her teachings do agree.

Sweet and Tender
Cora M. Owen

I have a mother who is kind,
  Her heart is loving too.
She shows me from the Word of
    God,
  Just what I ought to do.

She takes the time to talk with me,
  Though she has busy days.
She does so many things for me,
  In sweet and tender ways.

A Mother's Prayer
Wanda E. Brunstetter

Please, God, protect my children
    so dear,
Grant that they may have a
    listening ear.
May all their ways bring You
    glory
Because of examples in the Bible
    story.
May they always see Christ living
    in me,
For a Christian example is what I
    want to be.

She Cares
Dolores Steger

My mother cooks;
My mother cleans;
She buys the things I wear;
But, most of all,
She shows to me
Her love, attention, care.

Sugar Is Sweet
Dolores Steger

Sugar is sweet,
But Mother is sweeter.
Skating is neat,
But Mother is neater.
She's kind and she's loving,
I wish you could meet her.
And, as for a blessing,
There's none that can beat her.

Mother's Smile
Dolores Steger

I climb into my soft, warm bed;
On pillow then I lay my head;
I hear my mother say, "Sleep
    tight."
My light goes off; she says, "Good
    night."
Through nighttime, God will be
    with me
Till dawn when Mother's smile
    I'll see.

In the Merry
Month of May
Dolores Steger

In the merry month of May,
There's a special holiday.
When a tribute we can pay
To the one who guides our way
With such care, and so we say,
We love mom on Mother's Day
In the merry month of May.

Mother's Month
Helen Kitchell Evans

May is the mother month,
  The time of joyous birth
When warm sun falls gently
  And grass springs through the
    earth.

On the bough a bird sings
  Bringing joy to all to hear it;
His lusty chirping heals
  The tired and worn spirit.

What a merry month is May!
  Just the right time to say
We are grateful for all mothers
  On this special Mother's Day.

Millions of Mothers
Nell Ford Hann

Our Father God
  Made millions of stars
    To light up the entire sky.
Our Father God
  Made millions of birds
    With wings and will to fly.
Our Father God
  Made millions of grains
    Of sand in sugar white.
Our Father God
  Made millions of flowers
    With colors that delight.
Our Father God
  Made . . . everything,
From millions of things to a pre-
    cious few.
Our Father God
  Made millions of mothers
But only one for me—that is true.
  Happy Mother's Day—Mom!

Capital M
Dolores Steger

M is for memories I hold so dear,
And **M** is for moments whenever
    she's near;
M is for moral and masterful, too;
M is for modest and model, it's
    true;
I ponder these words when I
    think of another:
M with a capital **M** for my
    mother.

Mother's Love
Lillian Robbins

A mother's love can't be bought
  Or bargained for any way.
It seems to be there all the time
  And responds without delay.

My mother's love is full of glee.
  She makes my life worthwhile;
Her many hugs and trillion kisses
  And happy great big smile.

Someday when I become a
    woman,
  I'll look at all these years.
Then I'll know and understand
  Her laughter and her tears.

I want to learn much from her
  And be able to find my place.
So I can be a super mom;
  Bring smiles to my own child's
    face.

Grandma Knows
Christy L. Hoff

Who always has a peppermint or
　　two in her purse?
Who knows everyone in town,
　　How they're related,
　　Their better qualities and their
　　　worse?
　　　　Grandma does.

Who makes the best chicken
　　dumpling soup?
Who sees your picture in the
　　paper
　　Hears you on the radio,
　　Finds your part in the group?
　　　　Grandma can.

Who used Gramma's salve to heal
　　every hurt?
Who made family her work, her
　　hobby, her life?
Who took in a parade of children,
　　Loved them, helped wash
　　　away their dirt?
　　　　Grandma did.

Who knows the empty place left
　　behind?
Who knows the memories, the
　　peace, the love, that will fill
　　it?
Who knows the piece of her, left
　　with each of us.
　　As her spirit goes to be with
　　　Grandpa and with God?
　　　　Grandma knows,
　　　　　God knows!

Precious Mom
Lillian Robbins

Holy is the Father in Heaven;
Precious is my mom on earth.
Both of them are quite busy
And have been since my birth.

If Mom has undue worries,
She just turns to God above.
He always has the answer
And assures of His wonderful
　　love.

Life can be puzzling to humans,
And Mom fits right in line.
She says it's faith in God's power
Makes it all turn out just fine.

One thing special I've learned
　　already;
Love is the greatest of all.
God loves all His little children,
Lifts them up if they fall.

And it's Mom I can always cling to,
Cuddle up and share, even tears.
I know she loves me dearly
And has through all these years.

She proves it every day we're
　　together
As she cares and protects my life.
I hope to become a precious mom
And to my husband a loving wife.

By God's own special wisdom,
He made things just perfect for
　　me.
In my heart I'll hold Mom dearest
And love her forever; she'll see.

If You Think
Dixie Phillips

If you think I'm adorable and look really grand,
Just look at my mother! *(Points to mom in audience.)*
Let's give her a hand! *(Clap.)*
She's the one who curled my hair,
And told me just what I should wear!
She keeps our family in tip-top shape,
And even bought my brother a Superman cape! *(Let boy run down center
     aisle wearing Superman cape.)*
She makes me laugh when I'm real sad,
And once in a while makes my dad real mad!
Like the time she spent too much money,
My dad didn't think that was very funny! *(Shakes head no.)*
Now, I'm not saying that Dad can't make her mad!
But most of the time, he makes her glad!
Well, there was the time that he tried to escape
When he fixed a broken window with gray duct tape!
My mom screamed high-pitched and really loud,
Why, our house was surrounded by a crowd!
Dad said he thought she saw a mouse.
Boy, was there tension in our little house!
Mom made Dad throw all his duct tape away.
She said that's all she wanted for Mother's Day.
Well, it's like I told you—I'm sure you can see,
How proud my mother is of little ole me!
So on this very special occasion,
My "respect" to her I am raising!
I make a vow before you today,
May I never embarrass her by the words I say,
And may she be thrilled to hear me say,
I love you, Mom! Happy Mother's Day.

A Mother Knows

Dolores Steger

Why is it, do you suppose,
That a mother always knows?
She knows if you've been good or bad,
She knows when you are feeling sad,
She knows if homework you have done,
She knows when you are having fun,
She knows if you have washed your ears,
She knows when you have bedtime fears,
She knows if you have worries, cares,
She knows when you have said your prayers;
Why is it do you suppose,
A mother knows? I know God knows.

Meet Our Mothers

Iris Gray Dowling

(Each child can hold an 8 by 10 picture of his mother as he speaks.)

Child 1:   My mom stays near my side,
            Her thoughts for me will always abide.
Child 2:   My mother knows just when to share,
            By her life she shows how I should care.
Child 3:   My mother knows one thing for sure—
            She trusted Jesus as her Savior.
Child 4:   My mother isn't worried if we're poor;
            She says if we follow God we'll have much more.
Child 5:   My mother can always improvise,
            Because she looks to God who makes her wise.
Child 6:   My mother is my closest friend,
            My love for her will never end.

A Mother's Love

Dixie Phillips

(Two children—one a grandchild, the other dressed as a grandmother! She can be rocking in a rocking chair as the grandchild enters with her many questions. Children should use very expressive voices.)

Grandchild: I asked my Grandma one fine day,
"Will my mama's love for me ever go away?"

Grandma: Oh no, you silly little goose!
Your mama's love for you won't ever let you loose!

Grandchild: What if I did something to make her really mad?
Will she still love me even though she's soooo sad?

Grandma: Well, I'm sure you've got the power to make her cry
But she'll love you even past the day you die!

Grandchild: What if I broke her "most favorite" dishes?
And I didn't obey all her "most important" wishes?

Grandma: Well, I'm sure she'd have to recollect herself.
And remember people are more important than a dish on
a shelf!

Grandchild: What if one morning I just didn't mind?
And every word I said was unkind?

Grandma: Well, I'm sure she might feel like she'd want to skedaddle!
Then she'd probably go find her "most favorite" paddle.

Grandchild: Grandma, tell me just how do you know
That my mother will always love me so?

Grandma: Because I had a mother. I wasn't always this old!
And her love for me was worth far more than gold!

Grandchild: Oh, I think I'm beginning to see,
There's no end to my mother's love for me.

Grandma: That's right! The message is now quite clear.
Now, let's wish the mothers a happy Mother's Day this
year.

Grandchild: Whether you're young!

Grandma: Or whether you're old.

Unison: A mother's love is worth far more than gold!
Happy Mother's Day to each mother out there.
May God bless and keep you in His loving care.

To Mother, With Love

Iris Gray Dowling

Program Notes: Suggested songs have the author listed and can be found in the *Living Hymns*. Other words were created by this author for this occasion.

Announcer: We are glad you came today to share in a tribute to our mothers. Child 1 has a "A Mother's Day Wish" for all our mothers present.

Child 1: Now that Mother's Day is here again
    I have so much to say,
    But I can't find those fancy words
    To tell of mother's loving way,
    So let me say to every mother here—
    A great big "Happy Mother's Day."

Announcer: Our boys and girls are happy for mothers who love Jesus. We are glad you came to show your love for God and for your children today. Our younger children would like to sing about their love for Jesus and their mothers.

Preschool Group: "Jesus Loves Me" *(Sing stanza 1 and refrain followed by these words for mother. Use same tune.)* My mother loves me, my mother loves me, My mother loves me, that's why she's here today.

Announcer: Yes, the Bible tells us Jesus loves us and how He brought salvation to us. Because of His love we are blessed with Christian mothers who care so much about us. Six children are going to do an exercise spelling "MOTHER."

(Six children each hold a letter to spell MOTHER and recite the lines for that letter.)

M is for **Mother**
    Who gives so much for those God puts in her care.
O is for **Others**
    For whom she spends much time in prayer.
T is for **Tell**,
    She tells the Gospel story of God above.
H is for **Heart**,
    Where mother hides the verses of love.

E   is for **Eager**,
That's the way she works for everyone.
R   is for **Righteous**—
How God sees mother when she receives His Son.

Announcer: Child 8 thinks mother should be spelled with another letter. Let's see what it is.

Child 8 *(holds up an M)*: **M** stands for **Mother**
Turn it over and you will see, *(Turn M over to make W.)*
W stands for **Wonderful**,
That's how Mother is to me.

Announcer: We'll try not to forget to add the "W" next time. Some of our junior girls are going to sing "My Mother's Bible" by M. B. Williams.

Song: "My Mother's Bible"

Announcer: Wouldn't it be wonderful if everyone here today could look at their mother's Bible and see evidence of how much she studied it. Mothers who want to learn from the Bible also want to be better mothers so they can please the Lord. Six more children have an exercise titled "Let Us Tell About Our Mothers."

All: Let us tell you about our mothers.

Child 9: My mother is smart,
She has Jesus in her heart.

Child 10: My mother is beautiful to see,
But she lives the way God wants her to be.

Child 11: My mother works so hard each day,
Showing how to live the godly way.

Child 12: My mother teaches us God's holy Word,
She wants us to learn to love the Lord.

Child 13: My mother prepares us to live on this earth,
But to get us ready for Heaven, she tells us of the new birth.

Child 14: My mother has a heart full of love
Because she trusts the Savior above.

All: We love you, Mother!

Announcer: Now Child 15 wants us to know whose mom is the best. He'll recite "Why My Mom Is Best."

Child 15: Some moms have eyes of blue
Some have eyes of brown,
Mine has inner beauty
She deserves a crown. *(Presents his mom with a crown.)*

Announcer: All our children want to show appreciation for the love their mothers give every day. They will sing and then give something to each mother.

Song: "Oh, Do You Know My Mother Dear?" *(Use tune "Oh, Do You Know the Muffin Man?" They will sing all four stanzas and then repeat the fourth as they go from the platform and give flowers to their own mothers. Words for song as follows:)*

Stanza 1: Oh, do you know my mother dear, my mother dear, my mother dear, Oh, do you know my mother dear who loves me every day?

Stanza 2: Oh, yes, we know your mother dear, your mother dear, your mother dear, Oh, yes, we know your mother dear who loves you every day!

Stanza 3: Oh, where, oh, where is mother dear? Oh, where, oh, where is mother dear? Oh, where, oh, where is mother dear? I love you with all my heart.

Stanza 4: Oh, where, Oh, where is mother dear? Oh, where, oh, where is mother dear? Oh, where, Oh, where is mother dear? I need to find you now. *(Keep singing to give out flowers.)*

Announcer: That was a surprise, wasn't it? Child 16 wants to say thank you to his mother for "A Heart of Love."

Child 16: So many times when I think of my mother,
    I thank the heavenly Father above;
    That more than anything else,
    He gave my mother a heart of love.

Announcer: All the children will sing "O How I Love Jesus" by Frederick Whitfield.

Song: "Oh, How I Love Jesus" *(Refrain only.)*

Announcer: These boys and girls know how important it is to love Jesus, but they will change the words a little to honor their mothers today. Let's have all the mothers in the room stand up before we sing.

Song: "Oh, How I Love Mother" *(Same traditional tune.)*

Announcer: For our closing song let's all stand and sing "Jesus Loves Even Me" by Philip Bliss.

Father's Day

Welcome
Iris Gray Dowling

Welcome, everyone—
We're glad you came today.
We hope you'll feel the same,
When you hear the words we say.

Dad's Checkup
Iris Gray Dowling

Have you taken time to check
To see if you measure up?
How would you answer the
    heavenly Father
If He asked what kind of dad
    you've been?

A Truthful Dad
Iris Gray Dowling

I appreciate a dad like you
  Who always tells the truth;
I want to follow in your steps
  To help me be a Christian youth.

My Dad's Right
Iris Gray Dowling

There is a bright little kid,
  Who thinks you're always right.
He wants to be like you,
  So he watches day and night.

My Example
Iris Gray Dowling

Dad, you are the best!
  I love to hear you pray—
I love to go to church with you—
  You set a good example every
      day.

A Wise Dad
Iris Gray Dowling

There is no dad like mine—
  A man who's very wise—
Someone I can talk to
  When I need to be advised.

A Father's Prayer
Wanda E. Brunstetter

Dear heavenly Father, I'm sure
    You understand,
Because You are a father, and hold
    us in Your hand.
I pray that I may be a loving
    father too,
I want to follow Your example in
    all I say and do.
I ask for extra wisdom in know-
    ing what to say,
And may You bless my children
    on this special day.

Coolest Dad
Lillian Robbins

My dad loves me
I always see
    Even if I'm a little bad.

He corrects me so
But I really know
    He won't get way too mad.

It's his plan you see,
To carefully train me
    So I can grow up to be a man.

In spite of troubles
Or bursting bubbles,
    On my morals, I'll always
    stand.

Now in my fears
And even through tears,
    He helps me through the
    night.

I feel secure
And am pretty sure,
    My dad is always right.

Do I love my dad?
Does he make me glad?
    He's the coolest guy I know.

He hugs me tight
And whispers good night,
    And man, do I love him so!

Knight in Armor
Lillian Robbins

Of course he is all the world to
    me
    This super dad of mine.
He's my knight in brilliant armor;
    In my eyes he really shines.

He's the model that I look up to.
    He seems 'bout ten feet tall,
If I'm standing right beside him,
    Or see his picture on the wall.

He's so smart in every action,
    Answers questions when I ask.
He smiles and sings with gusto
    Even when he mows our grass.

What makes a dad so perfect?
    What he wears or where he
    works?
Or rather his love and
    companionship;
    How he sooths me when it
    hurts.

I just wish for all the kids,
    Every precious boy and girl,
If it's a dad to share a puzzle
    Or a baseball he would hurl.

If only everyone could have
    A dad who is just like mine,
Without a doubt, I'm positive
    They'd all turn out just fine.

Thank you Dad, for loving me
    Your willingness to always
    share.
To me you're sure the greatest
    Of all dads anywhere.

Internet Dad
Lillian Robbins

If I could choose a dad
  Through the internet or mail,
I'd scan through every web site
  And letters without fail.

I'd look for one whose tenderness
  Would be his normal pace,
A man who respects all others,
  Shows kindness in his face.

I'd want a dad to love me
  With his heart and with his soul.
He would shower me with caring
  When I'm young and when I'm
    old.

He may be rather handsome,
  But that really is not the test.
It's the way he shares with
    children
  That makes him be the best.

He would always be there for me
  To play or talk it through.
I would know he is really
    interested
  In everything I do.

He'd be sure to teach me Jesus
  And the good that God does
    bring.
Together we would worship,
  And joyfully we would sing.

My dad would hold me closely
  In the day or through the night.
He'd share my little problems,
  Help me know it's just all right.

Now as I consider all these things,
  It becomes perfectly clear,
I don't need to scan the internet,
  Such a one is with me here.

My dad is just the greatest
  All kids must feel that way.
And this is the perfect moment,
  To wish you all a wonderful
    Father's Day.

My Dear Grandpa
Nell Ford Hann

I'm as happy as a polka-dotted
    lark,
Blind as a bat when it's not in the
    dark;
Playful as a monkey, giddy as a
    clown,
And it's all because you are
    around.
When you're near I am walking
    on a cloud,
Strut like a peacock and twice as
    proud;
Sing like a bird in a sycamore
    tree,
'Cause you show me how things
    ought to be.
You help me with my cares of
    woe,
You tell me Jesus loves me so;
You're the best ole guy I ever saw,
And I love you true, my dear
    grandpa!

Just Like You Dad

Iris Gray Dowling

I have a wonderful dad,
He watches everything I do.
He cares if I've been bad or good,
And teaches me a lesson or two.
Someday I'll be all grown up,
And Dad, I want to be just like you.

Let's Tell About Our Fathers

Iris Gray Dowling

Child 1: My father has to have a lot of time,
   To hear the words I want to say.
Child 2: My father has to have a lot of patience,
   To help me learn my lessons each day.
Child 3: My father has to tell great stories,
   To make me happy and wise.
Child 4: My father has to be a good cook;
   He likes to fix the rolls that rise.
Child 5: My father has a sense of humor,
   Because I do such funny things.
Child 6: My dad is just a human being,
   Who doesn't think or act like he's a king.
Child 7: My father knows me inside out;
   He works so hard to get the things I need.
Child 8: My father tries to share his life;
   Things he teaches me I'll try to heed.
All: Thanks Dad, we appreciate you!

(Entire group or class can sing a Father's Day tribute. Suggested: "For the Beauty of the Earth" stanzas 1, 3, 5.)

Mary Adopts Mr. Brown

Helen Kitchell Evans

Characters: Two girls, Ashley and Mary; Mother; Mr. Brown

Setting: Optional. May have no setting with pretend action of opening
doors and going from room to room.

Ashley and Mary are walking slowly toward home from school.

Ashley: Here's old Mr. Brown's house. Shall we hurry by?
Mary: No, let's walk slowly and see if he's in the window.
Ashley: Everyone says that he's a mean, old grouch.
Mary: There he is. I'm going to wave. *(She does.)*
Ashley: Well, are you satisfied? He didn't wave to you, did he?
Mary: No, but he didn't wave his cane and shout at me like he has at
some of the children.
Ashley: I wonder why he's so mean?
Mary: I don't think he is really mean and grouchy. I think he is a very
lonely old man. He seems very unhappy.
Ashley: Maybe so. His wife died a few years ago. Maybe you are right.
Mary: I think that he has no one to love him. I'm going to adopt him.
Ashley: You're going to what?
Mary: Just what I said—adopt him.
Ashley: How can you do that? You mean legally?
Mary: No. I'm just going to think of him as another grandparent.
Ashley: That's a great idea. Well, here's your house. 'Bye. I'll see you
tomorrow.

(They separate. Ashley goes offstage. Mary enters house.)

Mother: Is that you, Mary? You are a little late. *(Coming into room.)*
Mary: I know. Ashley and I walked slowly and talked.
Mother: About what? Anything that you want to share?
Mary: It was about Mr. Brown. I feel sorry for him. It has been a long time
since anyone has seen him smile. If he knew about God, wouldn't he
smile?
Mother: I'm sure he knows about God, but sometimes when people are
sad and unhappy, they forget how much God can do for them.

Mary: I'm going to pray that God will help me make Mr. Brown smile.

Mother: Would you be willing to go to his house?

Mary *(hesitates)*: Well, I must admit I'm a little afraid, but God will help me I'm sure. I'm going to ask Mr. Brown to be my grandfather. It's been lonesome since my real grandpa died and with Father's Day coming up, I really miss Grandpa.

Mother: Yes, Dear, I know. I think you have a wonderful idea.

(Mary goes out and brings in a plate of cookies.)

Mary: I'm going right now. I'll take him the cookies that you made for me.

Mother: That's fine. *(Opens door for Mary then leaves stage.)*

(Mary walks to side and knocks on door.)

Mr. Brown *(gruffly)*: Who's out there?

Mary: It's Mary Lewis from down the street.

Mr. Brown *(still very loud and gruff)*: Well, what do you want?

Mary: I want you to be happy!

Mr. Brown *(opens door)*: You what? What do you want? *(Quieter now.)*

Mary: I brought you some cookies. I want you to be happy.

Mr. Brown *(grinning)*: I could do with a little happiness. Thank you for the cookies. Will you sit here on the porch and share them with me?

(Mary sits on the porch with Mr. Brown.)

Mary: You know Jesus loves you. That should make you happy. You shouldn't feel so sad. Will you be my adopted grandfather? You know my real grandfather died shortly after you lost your wife and with Father's Day coming up I really miss him.

Mr. Brown *(pats Mary's head)*: Dear child, God must have sent you to me. Sure I'll be your grandfather.

Mary: That's great! Will you wave to me each afternoon when I pass on my way home from school?

Mr. Brown: Yes, every afternoon. I'll be sitting close by the window.

Mary: I must go now. *(Hugs Mr. Brown.)* God loves you, Mr. Brown, and so do I.

Mr. Brown *(waving to Mary)*: Dear child, come again soon. You have made me a very happy old man.